The Highlands Of HEAVEN

THE MESSIAH AND HIS KINGDOM TO COME

"Your eyes will see the King in his beauty and the highlands of heaven."

~ *Isaiah 33:17* ~

by
Mark Baird

The Highlands of Heaven • The Messiah and His Kingdom to Come
Copyright © 2022 by Mark Baird

All rights reserved.

In accordance with the U.S. Copyright Act of 1976, no part of this publication may be reproduced, distributed, or transmitted in any form or by any means. The scanning, uploading, and electronic sharing of any part of this book without the permission of the publisher is unlawful piracy and theft of the author's intellectual property. If you would like to use material from this book (other than for review purposes), prior written permission must be obtained by contacting the publisher. Thank you for your support of the author's rights.

The Highlands of Heaven / Mark Baird
First Edition

Table of Contents

Introduction	5
Prophets and Prophecy	7
The Messiah's Reign	9
Who Is God?	20
Messiah, Maker, and Savior	22
Choose Life	27
Jews, and Gentiles (Non-Jews)	28
Babylon and End Times	32
The King of Babylon	35
Who Is 'Israel?'	37
New Testament Prophecy	42
Salvation	48
Faith	52
Repentance	55
Baptism	58
The End Times	60
The Tribulation	62
Final Things	67
About the Author	70

Introduction

The greatest and most wonderful event that will ever occur is about to happen. It has been promised and prophesied for thousands of years, and now, finally, it is about to happen! I overflow with excitement whenever I consider these amazingly marvellous things. I hope that you will too. Despite all the bad news that haunts us now, everything is going to be alright. Truth, goodness, and peace will indeed flourish upon our earth. Our world will be replenished and all of creation will rejoice. – This book is meant to inspire you and to give you a bright hope for tomorrow.

What will happen in our very near future? What things will occur within the lifetime of most people alive today? This book reveals to us the ultimate destination of this generation, and the events that will occur as this time-period concludes. We will enter a new age and a far better world that is to come.

Today, there are so many dire issues that are threatening our peace, economy, freedom, health, families, and even our very existence. The problems we are facing are so varied and immense that hope almost seems useless. – This book will change your mind. Yes, we will endure some difficult times ahead. But there is a new and wonderful world coming!

It seems that this revelation of God's return to earth one day has been the hope and expectation of all major religions since history began. In Hinduism there is the story of the god Vishnu coming back in the last cycle of time as a figure whose coming will look like a tremendous comet, riding a white horse and carrying a sword to destroy the forces of evil. And in Islam, the end of this age is referred to as *the Hour* and involves the Messiah returning to slay an evil, worldwide ruler, who has put the planet in peril. With this evil dictator out of the picture, a period of perfect harmony will ensue. -- And a myriad of indigenous religions also mention a Savior coming from heaven to bring peace and harmony to our world.

The Creator of Existence is coming back and bringing righteousness and peace to a cleansed and beautified new earth. -- The ancient prophets of all major faiths have made this prediction about the coming of a holy, heavenly ruler who will put an end to evil, and restore the earth to its fullest beauty. This righteous Ruler will descend to earth at just the right moment when all seems lost. He will triumph over evil and all who practice it. Those who eagerly receive Him will be blessed and welcomed into His earthly Kingdom. -- Judaism and Christianity refer to this divine being as the Messiah, and King of Kings and Lord of Lords. In the Bible, frequent mentions of this Holy Savior are described in magnificent details, unlike in anyother religious texts.

This purpose of this book is to give you strength and encouragement as we face the hard times coming upon us for awhile. But most importantly, my greatest desire is for you to get to know this coming Savior more intimately and to look forward with hope and expectancy for His coming.

May this book be a bright light for you and yours during the difficult days ahead that we must endure. For there is a magnificent world that is in our near future. A world God has prepared for those who seek Him and yearn for His reign on earth to begin.

Prophets and Prophecy

"This vision is for a future time. It describes the end, and it will be fulfilled. If it seems slow in coming, wait patiently, for it will surely take place. It will not be delayed."

~ Habakkuk 2:3 ~

As we follow and experience the major and significant world changing events that we are encountering now, we can have peace in the midst of the increasing violence and turbulent chaos seen across the world. All these things have been predicted in precise detail through prophets chosen by our Maker. Their words give us understanding as we watch world events unfold. They give us encouragement and hope in tough times. And they reveal to us the blessings we shall receive at His coming. -- He is coming soon! God in the flesh will rule this earth and bring worldwide peace.

Prophets are conduits of God so that they can share what He has to say to humankind. Therefore, we hear them speaking to us with direct quotations from our Creator. *"I am the LORD," he says, "and there is no other. I publicly proclaim bold promises. I do not whisper obscurities in some dark corner… I, the LORD, speak only what is true and declare only what is right…For there is no other God but me, a righteous God and Savior. There is none but me. Let all the world look to me for salvation!"* (Isaiah 45:18–21)

Again, our Creator insists, *"For I alone am God! I am God and there is none like me. Only I can tell the future before it happens. Everything I plan will come to pass."* (Isaiah 46:9–10)

These prophets took their calling very seriously. God instructed Moses that if a person claiming to be a prophet made a prophecy that was untrue that they were to be killed for speaking the word of God falsely. *"But the prophet who presumes to speak a word in my name that I have not commanded him to speak, or who speaks in the name of other gods, that same prophet shall die."* (Deuteronomy 18:20–22)

The inviolable sanctity of every word of the Bible and of its prophecies was established by Moses and has continued to this day. *"You shall not add unto the word which I command you, neither shall you diminish anything from it, that you may keep the commandments of the Lord your God which I command you."* (Deuteronomy. 4:2) As Believers we are assured that every promise given to those that God has chosen to be His prophets is true. These promises give us strength through the difficulties we endure while on this earth. We are comforted by these assurances. They enable us to persevere through trials and hardships. And they give us a bright hope for tomorrow. – There will come a day, and that day will come soon, when our Maker will descend from heaven and live on this earth as our Righteous Lord.

The Messiah's Reign

The Messiah will rule from Jerusalem in Israel when he returns. *"In the last days, Jerusalem and the Temple of the Lord will become the world's greatest attraction, and people from many lands will flow there to worship the Lord. "Come," everyone will say, "let us go up the mountain of the Lord, to the Temple of the God of Israel; there he will teach us his laws, and we will obey them." For in those days the world will be ruled from Jerusalem. The Lord will settle international disputes; all the nations will convert their weapons of war into implements of peace. Then at the last, all wars will stop, and all military training will end. O Israel, come, let us walk in the light of the Lord and be obedient to his laws!"* (Isaiah 2:2–5)

The curse upon mankind at the fall of Adam and Eve will be removed. *"Cursed is the ground because of you; through painful toil you will eat food from it all the days of your life. It will produce thorns and thistles for you, and you will eat the plants of the field. By the sweat of your brow you will eat your food until you return to the ground, since from it you were taken; for dust you are and to dust you will return."* (Genesis 3:16–19) With this curse removed, our bodies will remain healthy, and there will be no need for struggle to survive.

"On that day you will say, "Praise the Lord! He was angry with me, but now he comforts me. See, God has come to save me! I will trust and not be afraid, for the Lord is my strength and song; he is my salvation.

Oh, the joy of drinking deeply from the Fountain of Salvation!" In that wonderful day you will say, "Thank the Lord! Praise his name! Tell the world about his wondrous love. How mighty he is!" Sing to the Lord, for he has done wonderful things. Make known his praise around the world. Let all the people of Jerusalem shout his praise with joy. For great and mighty is the Holy One of Israel, who lives among you." (Isaiah 12:2–8)

Those who live within the city of Jerusalem will be especially blessed. But all peoples can enter the city, day and night. "***Listen to them singing! In that day the whole land of Judah will sing this song: "Our city is strong! We are surrounded by the walls of his salvation! Open the gates to everyone, for all may enter in who love the Lord. He will keep in perfect peace all those who trust in him, whose thoughts turn often to the Lord! Trust in the Lord God always, for in the Lord Jehovah is your everlasting strength.***" (Isaiah 26:1–4)

When this world has been restored and those who practice evil are removed, the Messiah, the King, will hold a worldwide feast. "***Here on Mount Zion in Jerusalem, the Lord Almighty will spread a wondrous feast for everyone around the world—a delicious feast of good food, with clear, well-aged wine and choice beef. At that time, he will remove the cloud of gloom, the pall of death that hangs over the earth; he will swallow up death forever. The Lord God will wipe away all tears and take away forever all insults and mockery against his land and people. The Lord has spoken—He will surely do it! In that day the people will proclaim, "This is our God in whom we trust, for whom we waited. Now at last he is here" What a day of rejoicing! For the Lord's good hand will rest upon Jerusalem.***" (Isaiah 25:6–10)

And we know what kind of a ruler he is and shall be: "***And he will be called: Wonderful Counselor, Mighty God, Everlasting Father, Prince of Peace. His government and its peace will never end. He will rule with fairness and justice from the throne of his ancestor David for all eternity. The passionate commitment of the Lord of Heaven's Armies will make this happen!***" (Isaiah 9:6–7)

"And the Spirit of the LORD will rest on him—the Spirit of wisdom and understanding, the Spirit of counsel and might, the Spirit of knowledge and the fear of the LORD. He will delight in obeying the LORD. He will not judge by appearance nor make a decision based on hearsay. He will give justice to the poor and make fair decisions for the exploited. The earth will shake at the force of his word, and one breath from his mouth will destroy the wicked. He will wear righteousness like a belt and truth like an undergarment." (Isaiah 11:1–5)

There will no longer be enmity between nations nor people. We will be united in one faith, one Lord, and one love. *"For as the waters fill the sea, so the earth will be filled with people who know the LORD. In that day the heir to David's throne will be a banner of salvation to all the world. The nations will rally to him, and the land where he lives will be a glorious place."* (Isaiah 11:9–10)

When the Lord returns there will be no more political parties and schisms and divisions among the people. They will be unnecessary. The anger that divides us will disappear. In its place will be harmony and justice. *"Look, a righteous king is coming! And honest princes will rule under him...until at last the Spirit is poured-out on us from heaven. Then the wilderness will become a fertile field, and the fertile field will yield bountiful crops. Justice will rule in the wilderness and righteousness in the fertile field. And this righteousness will bring peace. Yes, it will bring quietness and confidence forever. My people will live in safety, quietly at home. They will be at rest."* (Isaiah 32:1,15–18)

When the Messiah returns and establishes His throne in Jerusalem, everyone in the world will be eager to come and see Him and the beauty of his city. And its beauteous glory will cause our mouths to open and utter phrases of joy and thanksgiving! *"But the people of God will sing a song of joy, like the songs at the holy festivals. You will be filled with joy, as when a flutist leads a group of pilgrims to Jerusalem, the mountain of the LORD— to the Rock of Israel. And the LORD will make his majestic voice heard."* (Isaiah 30:29–30)

The Bible promises that the Messiah will come to Earth and reign as its King of Kings. It will be the most wonderful and glorious time that mankind has known since Adam and Eve in the Garden of God. All the Old Testament prophets refer to this new age. The prophecies we read are just a glimpse of what God has prepared for those who love him. When the Messiah comes, we will never be apart from Him again. And we will know true bliss. "*You will show me the way of life, granting me the joy of your presence and the pleasures of living with you forever.*" (Psalm 16:11)

This is how the prophet Daniel saw the coming of heaven's Holy One, "*I saw in a night vision, and behold, there came with the clouds of heaven one like unto a man, and he came even to the Ancient of Days, and they brought him before him. And there was given him dominion, and glory, and a kingdom, that all the peoples, nations, and languages should serve him: His dominion is an everlasting dominion, which shall not pass away, and his kingdom that which will never be destroyed.*" (Daniel 7:13)

All these prophecies will be fulfilled in the days to come in this generation. The time is not far off. Warnings about the destruction of our world are more real now than ever. We are in the last days of mankind's rule. It is almost the dawning of the Messiah's rule to begin. "*And when he comes, he will open the eyes of the blind and unplug the ears of the deaf. The lame will leap like a deer, and those who cannot speak will sing for joy! ... And a great road will go through that once deserted land. It will be named the Highway of Holiness. It will be only for those who walk in God's ways. ... Those who have been ransomed by the* LORD *will return. They will enter Jerusalem singing, crowned with everlasting joy. Sorrow and mourning will disappear, and they will be filled with joy and gladness.*" (Isaiah 35:5–10)

"*He shall judge between many peoples, and rebuke strong nations afar off; they shall beat their swords into plowshares, and their spears into pruning hooks; nation shall not lift-up sword against nation, nei-*

ther shall they learn war anymore. But everyone shall sit under his vine and under his fig tree, and no one shall make them afraid; for the mouth of the LORD of hosts has spoken." (Micah 4:1–4)

We who are alive when the Messiah returns will be joined by those who also believed in the Lord, lived accordingly, and died. *"**But those who die in the LORD will live; their bodies will rise again! Those who sleep in the earth will rise-up and sing for joy! For your life-giving light will fall like dew on your people in the place of the dead!**"* (Isaiah 26:19) --In whole and healthy bodies, we shall live on a perfect earth. *"**Then the eyes of the blind shall be opened, and the ears of the deaf shall be unstopped. Then the lame shall leap like a deer, and the tongue of the dumb sing. For waters shall burst forth in the wilderness, and streams in the desert.**"* (Isaiah 35:5–6)

Our world and its inhabitants, even all creation, shall live at peace. *"**The wolf also shall dwell with the lamb, the leopard shall lie down with the young goat, the calf and the young lion and the fatling together; and a little child shall lead them. The cow and the bear shall graze; their young ones shall lie down together; and the lion shall eat straw like the ox. The nursing child shall play by the cobra's hole, and the weaned child shall put his hand in the viper's den. They shall not hurt nor destroy in all My holy mountain, for the earth shall be full of the knowledge of the Lord as the waters cover the sea.**"* (Isaiah 11:6–9)

The Lord will not rule as earthly monarchs. This is the supreme Son of God. He will not only bring about world peace and keep it, He will also restore the earth to more beauty than ever before. He will rule with the strength and wisdom of God Almighty. Our bodies will no longer desire what grieves the Lord. We shall be made holy. *"**But in that day, the branch of the LORD will be beautiful and glorious; the fruit of the land will be the pride and glory of all who survive in Israel. All who remain in Zion will be a holy people... Then the LORD will provide shade for Mount Zion and all who assemble there. He will provide a canopy of** *cloud during the day and smoke and flaming fire at night, covering the glorious land. It will be a shelter from daytime heat and be a hiding place from storms and rain.*" (Isaiah 4:2–6)

Most people have anxiety about the hardships that we are entering into now, global warming, unceasing wars, political and societal upheavals, and the fall of the rule of law. But we are given hope. This time of trial and tribulation will not last. "*Nevertheless, that time of darkness and despair will not go on forever…There will be a time in the future when Galilee of the Gentiles, which lies along the road that runs between the Jordan and the sea, will be filled with glory. The people who walk in darkness will see a great light. For those who live in a land of deep darkness, a light will shine.*" (Isaiah 9:1–3)

Instead of annihilation, we will be blessed with a loving, caring Maker, who formed us to be His forever! The earth will be inhabited by people who love the Lord and eachother. We will live in peace and harmony with our neighbors. And there will be no evil or death.

The powerful, fallen angel, Satan, who has hated mankind and God's Messiah from the beginning, will be no more. There will no longer be our Tempter and Destroyer to plague us. "*How you are fallen from heaven, O Lucifer, son of the morning! How you are cut down to the ground, you who weakened the nations! For you have said in your heart… 'I will ascend above the heights of the clouds, I will be like the Most High.' Those who see you will gaze at you, and consider you, saying: 'Is this the man who made the earth tremble, who shook kingdoms, who made the world as a wilderness and destroyed its cities, who did not open the house of his prisoners?*" (Isaiah 14:12, 16–17)

We are encouraged by such promises to endure and to persevere in doing good. The earth will bear food for all abundantly, and we shall be full of joy! And all human infirmities will disappear. "*Soon—and it will not be very long—the forests of Lebanon will become a fertile field, and the fertile field will yield bountiful crops. In that day* the deaf will hear words read from a book, and the blind will see through the gloom and darkness. The humble will be filled with fresh joy from the LORD. The poor will rejoice in the Holy One of Israel." (Isaiah 29:17–19)

The earth and its soil will also rejoice and be carpeted with flowers *"Even the wilderness and desert will be glad in those days. The wasteland will rejoice and blossom with spring crocuses. Yes, there will be an abundance of flowers and singing and joy! The deserts will become as green as the mountains of Lebanon, as lovely as Mount Carmel or the plain of Sharon. There the LORD will display his glory, the splendor of our God."* (Isaiah 35:1–4)

"Look! I am creating new heavens and a new earth, and no one will even think about the old ones anymore. Be glad; rejoice forever in my creation!" (Isaiah 65:17)

"As surely as my new heavens and earth will remain, so will you always be my people, with a name that will never disappear," says the LORD." (Isaiah 66:22)

The entire Bible is florid with beautiful promises about what God has in store for those that seek Him earnestly. We cannot withhold from those we care about this wonderful news! *"With this news, strengthen those who have tired hands, and encourage those who have weak knees. Say to those with fearful hearts, "Be strong, and do not fear, for your God is coming to destroy your enemies. He is coming to save you."* (Isaiah 35:3–4)

"O Zion, messenger of good news, shout from the mountaintops! Shout it louder, O Jerusalem. Shout, and do not be afraid. Tell all the towns... "Your God is coming!" Yes, the Sovereign LORD is coming in power. He will rule with a powerful arm. See, he brings his reward with him as he comes. He will feed his flock like a shepherd. He will carry the lambs in his arms, holding them close to his heart. He will gently lead the mother sheep with their young." (Isaiah 40:9–11)

When the Lord of Heaven comes to live with us upon this earth, every eye on earth will see his coming. Suddenly, the earth will be filled with brilliant light and with the voices of millions of angels singing his praise. *"His brilliant splendor fills the heavens, and the earth is filled with his praise. His coming is as brilliant as the sunrise. Rays of light flash from his hands, where his awesome power is hidden... He is the Eternal One!"* (Habakkuk 3:3–4,6)

"Suddenly, the glory of the God of Israel appeared from the east. The sound of his coming was like the roar of rushing waters, and the whole landscape shone with his glory." (Ezekiel 43:2)

Until this glorious time occurs, we have work to do. We are to be the Messiah's ambassadors to the world. We are to live now, as we will then, in perfect love, harmony, and righteousness. *"And it is he who says, "I, the* Lord, *have called you to demonstrate my righteousness. I will take you by the hand and guard you, and I will give you to my people, Israel, as a symbol of my covenant with them. And you will be a light to guide the nations. You will open the eyes of the blind. You will free the captives from prison, releasing those who sit in dark dungeons. "I am the* Lord; *that is my name!"* (Isaiah 42:6–8)

Our Lord is not a harsh ruler. Just the opposite. He looks upon us with great compassion, understanding, patience and love. *"Look at my servant, whom I strengthen. He is my chosen one, who pleases me. I have put my Spirit upon him. He will bring justice to the nations. He will not shout or raise his voice in public. He will not crush the weakest reed or put out a flickering candle* (the meek and mild). *He will bring justice to all who have been wronged. He will not falter or lose heart until justice prevails throughout the earth. Even distant lands beyond the sea will wait for his instruction."* (Isaiah 42:1–4)

All our misery, regrets, hurts, and sadness will vanish. *"To all who mourn in Israel he will give a crown of beauty for ashes, a joyous blessing instead of mourning, festive praise instead of despair. In their righteousness, they will be like great oaks that the* Lord *has planted for his own glory."* (Isaiah 61:3)

Instead of anxiety and worry, we will experience an everlasting river of joy flowing from our hearts *"Those who have been ransomed by the* Lord *will enter Jerusalem singing, crowned with everlasting joy. Sorrow and mourning will disappear, and they will be filled with joy and gladness."* (Isaiah 51:11) And *"You will live in joy and peace. The mountains and hills will burst into song, and the trees of the field will clap their hands!"* (Isaiah 55:12)

"I will make peace your leader and righteousness your ruler. Violence will disappear from your land; the desolation and destruction of war will end. Salvation will surround you like city walls, and praise will be on the lips of all who enter there. "No longer will you need the sun to shine by day, nor the moon to give its light by night, for the Lord *your God will be your everlasting light, and your God will be your glory. Your days of mourning will come to an end."* (Isaiah 60:17–20)

We will all be good people without selfishness, lust, fleshly desires, and sin. And we will flourish and prosper. *"All your people will be righteous. They will possess their land forever, for I will plant them there with my own hands in order to bring myself glory. The smallest family will become a thousand people, and the tiniest group will become a mighty nation. At the right time, I, the* Lord, *will make it happen."* (Isaiah 60:20–22)

For those of us who have been estranged from others and never a part of a large loving family or a group of friends, we will never be lonely again. We will belong and be united with one love and desire. And all the while, our God who loves us immensely and sweetly, will be continually blessing us with more! *"They will be my people, and I will be their God. And I will give them one heart and one purpose: to worship me forever, for their own good and for the good of all their descendants. And I will make an everlasting covenant with them: I will never stop doing good for them. I will put a desire in their hearts to worship me, and they will never leave me. I will find joy doing good for them and will faithfully and wholeheartedly replant them in this land."* (Jeremiah 32:38–41)

These will be the words we utter in amazement to ourselves and to eachother, "*I am overwhelmed with joy in the LORD my God! For he has dressed me with the clothing of salvation and draped me in a robe of righteousness. I am like a bridegroom dressed for his wedding or a bride with her jewels.*" (Isaiah 61:10)

And until this time dawns upon the earth, we are to busy ourselves with this divine task, "*The LORD has sent this message to every land:* "*Tell the people who seek me, 'Look, your Savior is coming. See, he brings his reward with him as he comes.*" *They will be called "The Holy People" and "The People Redeemed by the LORD.*" (Isaiah 62:11–12) – And while doing so, we are to live a circumspect life. "*This is what the LORD says: "Be just and fair to all. Do what is right and good, for I am coming soon to rescue you and to display my righteousness among you. Blessed are all those who are careful to do this.*" (Isaiah 56:1–2)

"*Then I will sprinkle clean water on you, and you will be clean. Your filth will be washed away, and you will no longer worship idols. And I will give you a new heart, and I will put a new spirit in you. I will take out your stony, stubborn heart and give you a tender, responsive heart. And I will put my Spirit in you so that you will follow my decrees and be careful to obey my regulations. "And you will live in Israel, the land I gave your ancestors long ago. You will be my people, and I will be your God. I will cleanse you of your filthy behavior. I will give you good crops of grain, and I will send no more famines on the land. I will give you great harvests from your fruit trees and fields.*" (Ezekiel 36:25–30)

Life is not to be lived only in search of comfort, fun, and pleasure. We each have a much higher call to our existence. We are to live to please our Maker, the Messiah. Those who ignore this and reject a life of faith and good deeds will face a fearful moment when they are called before God's throne. "*I watched as thrones were put in place and the Ancient One sat down to judge. His clothing was as white as snow, his hair like purest wool. He sat on a fiery throne with wheels of blazing fire, and a river of fire was pouring out, flowing from his presence. Millions of angels ministered to him; many millions stood to attend him... As my vision continued that night, I saw someone like a son of man coming with the clouds of heaven. He approached the Ancient One and was led into his presence. He was given authority, honor, and sovereignty over all the nations of the world, so that people of every race and nation and language would obey him. His rule is eternal—it will never end. His kingdom will never be destroyed. Then the court began its session, and the books were opened."* (Daniel 7:13–14)

We are God's beloved ones because we believe. We will even be spiritually married to our Lord. *"When that day comes," says the LORD, "you will call me 'my husband' instead of 'my master.' ...On that day I will make a covenant with all the wild animals and the birds of the sky and the animals that scurry along the ground so they will not harm you. I will remove all weapons of war from the land so you can live unafraid in peace and safety. I will make you my wife forever, showing you righteousness and justice, unfailing love and compassion. I will be faithful to you and make you mine, and you will finally know me as the LORD."* (Hosea 2:16,18–20)

Who Is God?

There are many religions. Most believe in a Creator who formed the universe and who desires to have an eternal, loving relationship with all of us. Their concepts of this God and what He desires for us are similar too: He insists on us loving him above all else and modifying our behavior to align with His will, which we express by acts of love.

God has these three distinct attributes: He is **Omnipresent**. God is fully present everywhere in the entire Cosmos at the same time! That means that wherever and whoever we are God hears your prayers. -- How can the Lord of Heaven hear all the words lifted to him from across the world separately, and answer each one uniquely? He can because he is personally present with everyone whenever we lift-up our heart and voice to Him. "*I am a God who is everywhere and not in one place only. No one can hide where I cannot see them. Do you not know that I am everywhere in heaven and on earth?*" (Jeremiah 23:23–24)

God is **Omniscient**. He contains all the knowledge of everything. The Bible teaches us that: "*God hears our thoughts before we think them, knows our words before we speak them, and sees what we do before we do it. There is nothing we know that he does not. Nothing is hidden from Him.*" (Psalm 139) -- God knows all.

"*Have you never heard? Have you never understood? The LORD is the everlasting God, the Creator of all the earth. He never grows weak or weary. No one can measure the depths of his understanding.*" (Isaiah 40:28)

God is **Omnipotent**. He is the source of all power, energy, force, and life. He is the Creator who established existence upon universal laws. He is the all-knowing and all-powerful being who designed it all. "*For the LORD is God, and he created the heavens and earth and put everything in place. He made the world to be lived in, not to be a place of empty chaos. "I am the LORD," he says, "and there is no other."* (Isaiah 45:18)

But above all else, God is Love. In fact, the very meaning of God's name is love. "*The LORD passed in front of Moses, calling out (his name), "Yahweh! The LORD! The God of compassion and mercy! I am slow to anger and filled with unfailing love and faithfulness.*" (Exodus 34:6) This is how God loves us, and it is how we who seek Him must love all others too, with unfailing love, compassion, and mercy.

God knows those who love Him, and who love others in the same way. We cannot fool Him. The purpose for this temporary life on this temporary earth is for us to prove our love for Him. For we are promised that if we seek God earnestly that we will be rewarded. "*Behold, the Lord GOD comes with might, and His arm establishes His rule. His reward is with Him, and His recompense accompanies Him. He tends His flock like a shepherd; He gathers the lambs in His arms and carries them close to His heart. He gently leads the nursing ewes.*" (Isaiah 40:10–11)

Our Creator made us to be His children that he can delight in and bless. That is why our earth is unique in all creation. This is where He has chosen to reside and to reign forever, while enjoying the presence of those who delight in Him and in whom He delights too. -- Even with our most amazing telescopes we cannot find any place like earth. This place is special. It is where God has chosen to live with those who he loves and who love Him forever. "*God, the LORD, created the heavens and stretched them out. He created the earth and everything in it. He gives breath to everyone, life to everyone who walks the earth.*" (Isaiah 42:5)

"*I am the one who made the earth and created people to live on it. With my hands I stretched out the heavens. All the stars are at my command.*" (Isaiah 45:12)

Messiah, Maker, and Savior

The belief that one day our Creator will come and live among us on earth is believed by most of the world's major religions, and by a myriad of indigenous religions too. But only in the Jewish and Christian bibles do we find a wealth of descriptive and explanatory scripture about the Messiah.

The ultimate destiny of mankind is not the world we live in now. This world is saturated with violence, misery, suffering, and death. No. God has planned a far, far better future for us. One day soon, all who believe in the Messiah, living devout lives and looking forward to his coming, will be given perfect, eternal bodies and enjoy a world that will never end and be full of splendor, joy, peace, and beauty. – And for that to happen, those who live there must be perfect too. There will be no sin or evil. And that too, is what the Messiah will do for us. He will make us perfect.

According to the Old Testament prophets, the Messiah will come two times; once as a sacrifice for our sins, and then again to establish his worldwide kingdom. Before he can usher in his kingdom, he first needs to prepare a people to share it with him. And so, at his first advent he came to reveal God's love for us that we would know Him, trust Him, and believe in Him. He came to give us this knowledge that cleanses our hearts and souls. He is holy and lives in perfection and glory. And so, the Messiah did for us that which we could not do for ourselves. -- The prophets all agree: The Messiah paid the penalty for our sins himself, in order to remove sin's wall of separation that divides us. *"For he was cut off from the land of the living; for the transgression of my people he was punished."* (Isaiah 53:8)

This is an amazing and most wonderful event! To avoid being separate from humankind and to reconcile our sinful selves to Himself, the Messiah, suffered rejection and death in our place. *"After he has suffered, he will see the light of life and be satisfied; by his knowledge my righteous servant will justify many, and he will bear their iniquities… because he poured out his life unto death and was numbered with the transgressors* (sinners). *For he bore the sin of many and made intercession for the transgressors."* (Isaiah 53:11–12)

It is by this tremendous show of the Messiah's love for us that we have been made right with God. *"But he was pierced for our transgressions, he was crushed for our iniquities; the punishment that brought us peace was on him, and by his wounds we are healed."* (Isaiah 53: 5) This was not anything we could have done for ourselves. The Messiah, the Lord and the Creator of heaven and earth, became flesh and died for us so that we can be forgiven. -- This was metaphorically demonstrated when the Moses led the Jews out of Egypt and the first Passover was initiated. *"At the time appointed for their deliverance from Egyptian bondage, the Lord commanded each family in Israel to sacrifice a lamb, to sprinkle its blood on their doorposts."* Their instructions were to splash the blood on the top and on both sides of their home's door, in the shape of a cross. They then put the remaining blood in a bowl at the foot of the door. *"When the LORD goes through the land to strike down the Egyptians, he will see the blood on the top and sides of the doorframe and will pass over that doorway, and he will not permit the destroyer to enter your houses and strike you down."* – The Messiah came first as our Passover Lamb. – When He comes again, it will be as our Deliverer, and King.

The lamb represents innocence and purity. The sinless died in the place of sinners. – This was an example of what the Messiah would someday come and do for them, and for the entire world. He became the sacrificial lamb. – This was also foretold when God tested Abraham's faith and he was asked to take his son Isaac and to sacrifice him on an alter. On the way, his young son asked, "*The fire and wood are here," Isaac said, "but where is the lamb for the burnt offering?*" (Genesis 22:7) Then his father, Abraham replied, "*God himself will provide the lamb for the burnt offering, my son.*" (Genesis 22:8) Abraham obeyed the Lord and took his son to the mountain. By his faith in God's mercy and love, he was confident that God would provide a substitute. And because of this faith of Abraham's, this promise was given, "*I will surely bless you and make your descendants as numerous as the stars in the sky and as the sand on the seashore. Your descendants will take possession of the cities of their enemies, and through your offspring all nations on earth will be blessed, because you have obeyed me.*" (Genesis 22:17–18) – And indeed, all the people of this earth have been blessed through Abraham's offspring, the Messiah! -- Isaac was Abraham's only son with his wife Sarah. And Abraham was well over the age of 100 when this occurred. He would not have any more children. --Therefore, because of God's promise to bless Abraham's "offspring" Abraham knew that even if his son was sacrificed, God would raise Isaac up to live again.

So, since the Messiah, the Savior of the world, substituted himself for us and bore the penalty of our sins as our Passover lamb, is all of mankind now saved from being judged for their sins?

The answer to this question is also given in the story of the Jews escape from Egypt on their way to the promised land. On their way through the desert it says, "*But the people grew impatient on the way; they spoke against God and against Moses.*" (Numbers 21:4) Instead of being thankful for God's deliverance from slavery, and being taken to a land "flowing with milk and honey," they complained, "*Why have you brought us up out of Egypt to die in the wilderness?*" (Numbers 21:5) In response to the peoples' rebellion against God, "*Then the LORD sent venomous snakes among them; they bit the people and many Israelites died. The people *came to Moses and said, "We sinned when we spoke against the LORD and against you. Pray that the LORD will take the snakes away from us." So, Moses prayed for the people.*" (Numbers 21:6–7) – Everyone was dying from being bitten by poisonous snakes, just as everyone is also bitten with the desire to rebel against God's will and to sin. So, Moses called out to God to forgive them and to heal them! And this is how God answered his prayer, "*The LORD said to Moses, "Make a snake and put it up on a pole; anyone who is bitten can look at it and live. So, Moses made a bronze snake and put it up on a pole. Then when anyone was bitten by a snake and looked at the bronze snake, they lived.*" (Numbers 21:8–9) And in like manner, one day the Messiah would also be lifted-up on a pole. And all those who look to that immense sacrifice and honor it will also be saved from the poison of sin and live too.

Because the Messiah stood in our place and received the punishment we deserve, He is also our Priest and our Savior, by which those who believe are forgiven for their sins and saved from God's wrath.

Anyone who is honest with their self knows that they have done things that are wrong, hurtful, and selfish. Although we do some good things, we also lie, steal, curse, cheat, hate, and abuse others. None of us is without fault. It is our human nature to protect and to provide for our own needs before the needs of others. – As David said in this psalm, "***None is righteous, no, not one; no one understands; no one seeks for God. All have turned aside; together they have become worthless: no one does good, not even one.***" (Psalm 14:3) – Even the best of us has faults and fails to always be loving, kind, and merciful.

God knows who we are and how we are made. None of us is perfect and entirely righteous. And so, he sent His Son, to pay the penalty of our sins and to repair our relationship with our Maker. God is holy. And those who enter His eternal kingdom must be holy too. So, we have this beautiful assurance from Isaiah, "***Come now, let us settle the matter,***" says the LORD. "***Though your sins are like scarlet, they shall be as white as*** *snow; though they are red as crimson, they shall be like wool.*" (Isaiah 1:18) – And our proper response we are told by King David in a psalm, "*Serve the LORD with fear and celebrate his rule with trembling. Kiss his Son, or he will be angry, and your way will lead to your destruction, for His wrath can flare up in a moment. Blessed are all who take refuge in him.*" (Psalm 2:11–12)

Another name given to the Messiah is "*the son of David.*" This means that in human lineage the Messiah will come from the same tribe as King David. But in 596 B.C King Nebuchadnezzar of Babylon destroyed Jerusalem and ended the Davidic line of ascension to the throne. However, Isaiah gave this prophetic promise to the Jewish people taken into exile and slavery. Someday, God will send another King, who will also be from David's line. "*The royal line of David will be cut off, chopped down like a tree; but from the stump will grow a Shoot—yes, a new Branch from the old root. And the Spirit of the Lord shall rest upon him, the Spirit of wisdom, understanding, counsel, and might; the Spirit of knowledge and of the fear of the Lord. His delight will be obedience to the Lord. He will not judge by appearance, false evidence, or hearsay, but will defend the poor and the exploited. He will rule against the wicked who oppress them. For he will be clothed with fairness and with truth.*" (Isaiah 11:1–3)

The Messiah, God's Son, is coming to rule this earth in righteousness. There will be no more quarreling and corrupt politicians seeking after personal gain and power rather than the good and welfare of the people. In their place, we will be ruled by the Lord of Heaven and Earth.

Here is how the Messiah proclaimed his purpose. "*The Spirit of the Lord is on me, because he has anointed me to proclaim good news to the poor. He has sent me to proclaim freedom for the prisoners and recovery of sight for the blind, to set the oppressed free, to proclaim the year of the Lord's favor.*" (Isaiah 61:1)

Choose Life

Throughout the Bible we are told of God's ultimate plans. He has made us to have a relationship with Him that will last forever. He created us and the earth for the purpose of his sifting through humanity to find those that desire goodness, and who desire to practice love, humility, kindness, and generosity. These are those who will enjoy the wonderful new world He has promised for all who seek Him.

Our Creator declares his love for us repeatedly throughout the Bible. And just as any good father, He attempts to shape our characters and to give us healthy, happy, purpose-filled lives. But ultimately it is up to us. *"See, I set before you today life and death. Choose life! Love the Lord your God, walk in obedience to him, and keep his commands; then you will live and increase, and the LORD your God will bless you."* (Deuteronomy 30:15–16)

The prophet Moses gave us the Ten Commandments and God's laws, the standard of conduct for all who believe and trust Him. They instruct us how to live a life that pleases the Lord. *"More to be desired are they than Gold, more than much fine gold. By them your servant is warned; in keeping them there is great reward."* (Psalm 19)

As you read these wonderful and glorious descriptions of the reign of the Messiah on our replenished earth, take hope and be encouraged. We are getting very close to the end of the rule of fallen mankind and the ushering in of a new and marvellous age.

Jews, and Gentiles (Non-Jews)

Before I share more wonderful descriptions of our glorious future, I need to explain how non-Jews fit into these promises that we are reading. The books of Moses and the prophets were written to the Jews, and for those living within Israel and Judah. But along with the many foretold blessings for Jews, there are also verses that assure "Gentiles" (non-Jews) that these promises are for them too. – We are told as early as the first book of the Bible, "*The LORD had said to Abram, "Go from your country, your people and your father's household to the land I will show you. "I will make you into a great nation, and I will bless you; I will make your name great, and you will be a blessing. I will bless those who bless you, and whoever curses you I will curse; and all peoples on earth will be blessed through you.*" (Genesis 12:1–3) – Anyone who also believes in the God of Abraham, and joins with those who do, will receive the same blessings as those promised to the Jews.

Even in ancient times, non-Jews could become Jews and receive every blessing of those people. *"And when a stranger shall sojourn with thee and will keep the Passover to the Lord… he shall be as one that is born in the land."* – (Exodus 12:48)

David's son, Solomon, when dedicating the magnificent Temple he built for the Lord, included gentiles in his prayer too. *"Also concerning*

28 | Mark Baird

the foreigner who is not of Your people Israel, when he comes from a far country for Your name's sake (for they will hear of Your great name and Your mighty hand, and of Your outstretched arm); when he comes and prays toward this house, hear in heaven Your dwelling place, and do according to all for which the foreigner calls to You, in order that all the peoples of the earth may know Your name, to fear You, as do Your people Israel, and that they may know that this house which I have built is called by Your name." (1 Kings 8:41–43)

And Isaiah repeats this assurance given by the Lord to every nation and race on Earth, *"Also the foreigners who join themselves to the Lord, to minister to Him, and to love the name of the Lord, to be His servants, every one who keeps from profaning the sabbath and holds fast My covenant; even those I will bring to My holy mountain and make them joyful in My house of prayer. Their burnt offerings and their sacrifices will be acceptable on My altar; for My house will be called a house of prayer for all the peoples."* The Lord God, who gathers the dispersed of Israel, declares, *"Yet others I will gather to them, to those already gathered."* (Isaiah 56:6–8)

The Jewish people have been sorely persecuted all over this world. These people are God's chosen race. His prophets, the Bible, and the Messiah, all come from this special race. Our God always defends and lifts-up the weakest, the smallest, and the ones who endure persecution. Certainly, this has been the history of the Jewish people. They have never had much peace on this earth. And the history of the Christian Church is abominable in their treatment of Jews. This is very unfortunate. For Jews more than all peoples on earth are God's chosen. Those who bless them will be blessed, and those that curse them will be cursed. *"But the LORD will have mercy on the descendants of Jacob. He will choose Israel as his special people once again. He will bring them back to settle once again in their own land. And people from many different nations will come and join them there and unite with the people of Israel. The nations of the world will help the people of Israel to return, and those who come to live in the LORD's land will serve them."* (Isaiah 14:1–2)

There will be a great worldwide revival among the Jewish people in the last days of this current age. It is prophesied about many times. Their eyes will be opened, and they will know their Messiah and their Savior. They shall return to Israel and Judah, the lands promised to them through Moses. And when they return, they shall sing this song: "*In that day, everyone in the land of Judah will sing this song: "Our city is strong! We are surrounded by the walls of God's salvation. Open the gates to all who are righteous; allow the faithful to enter. You will keep in perfect peace all who trust in you, all whose thoughts are fixed on you!*" (Isaiah 26:1–3)

As we read the Old Testament, it is not merely a bunch of laws and regulations. It contains the history of God's relationship with the Jewish race, which He created through Abraham, Isaac, and Jacob.

Joseph was a son of Jacob who became the Regent of Egypt and handled the administration of all Egypt. In return, he and his family were given Egypt's most fertile area for 430 years, the 'Land of Goshen.' Their lineage grew to number millions while living in Egypt's most fertile area. But after so many centuries, the Egyptian population grew too, until they coveted the land where the foreign Jewish people still lived. Their land was taken away, and then the Jews became slaves and were harshly treated. That is when God called Moses to rescue them and take them to the "Promised Land." That place is modern day Israel, the most special place on earth to God. And Jerusalem is where his earthly throne will reside.

Joshua led the people into the land promised by God. It took generations before they were able to eradicate or subdue the many other tribes and nations that were established there. It was King David who truly established Israel and Judah as nations. He expanded their territory and became a primary force in the Middle East. For all his successes he praised God, as we read in his Psalms. But later generations, and the kings who ruled them, were often more attracted to the idolatry and the pantheon of gods worshipped by the nations around them. The Jewish nation became polluted with temples and worshippers of false gods. They began sacrificing children to demon idols and practicing perverted rituals. Pagan temples became houses of prostitution for men and women. Even within the Temple built by Solomon, David's son, it was defaced with idols and immoral graffiti. – That was why God continued to send prophets: to warn the people to repent, or else their nation would be taken away and they would become slaves to another people. -- The nation of Babylon and its king, Nebuchadnezzer, were used by God to finally bring the punishment about which, for decades, Israel and Judah had been warned.

Just as the prophet Jeremiah had prophesied before their captivity and exile, after 70 years, a remanent chose to return, when permitted by Cyrus of Persia, who had defeated Babylon. *"This whole country will become a desolate wasteland, and these nations will serve the king of Babylon seventy years."* (Jeremiah 25:11) – And Daniel, who was serving in Babylon still, 70 years later, remembered this promise. Daniel wrote: *"In the first year of Darius the son of Ahasuerus ... I, Daniel, understood by the books the number of the years specified by the word of the LORD through Jeremiah the prophet, that He would accomplish seventy years in the desolations of Jerusalem."* (Daniel 9:1-2)

"This is what the LORD says: "When seventy years are completed for Babylon, I will come to you and fulfill my good promise to bring you back to this place." (Jeremiah 29:10) Indeed, Jewish captives were released, and Jews returned to Jerusalem, which was in shambles with hardly a stone left upon another. Then they began rebuilding of the city and the Temple.

The prophecies given by prophets are promises made by the God Almighty. They always come to pass. *"My word that goes out from my mouth: It will not return to me empty; but will accomplish what I desire and achieve the purpose for which I sent it."* (Isaiah 55:11)

Babylon and End Times

Certainly, some of the most precise details of the first and the second advent of the Messiah's coming to Earth are described in the Book of Daniel. Please be patient as I digress into some history in order to properly explain our future.

Babylon was an immense kingdom that had gathered and hoarded the riches of the all the nations surrounding them between 600 and 500 BC. They were a people who practiced sorcery and magical arts. And they had multiple gods that they worshipped. Hence, from the time of the Jewish captivity there, the name '*Babylon*' has referred to much more than the capital city of King Nebuchadnezzar, or the city in Iraq. It became a metaphor for all worldly evils, the vain seeking for fleshly pleasures, and the delving into spiritual powers and practices forbidden by God, that entice humanity. And so, from the prophet Isaiah to Malachi we are warned about this materialistic whore, "Babylon," who seduces the world and draws them away from Truth and from worshipping the true and Holy God.

In 587 B.C. Nebuchadnezzar entered Jerusalem after a lengthy siege. He murdered and enslaved its inhabitants and every Jew within the land. Some of the elite Jewish young men were enrolled in various schools to train them to be officials in the Babylonian court. The young prophet Daniel was one. He was trained as a wiseman to counsel the king. And it is in the Book of Daniel that we learn of many tremendous prophecies about the future, and about the time in which we now live.

The first vision given to Daniel was a vision of the future greatest kingdoms of world until the advent of the Messiah's second coming as the King of Kings. This vision was given to the King of Babylon, Nebuchadnezzar, during the Jews exile there. But he could not understand its meaning. He demanded that his court wise men tell him. And to make sure that they told him the truth, he required them to read his mind and to describe the details of his dream without it being told to them. Of course, they could not. And in frustrated rage, Nebuchadnezzar was about to kill all his wisemen, until the prophet Daniel, who had been chosen to become a wiseman too, prayed, and God told him the dream and its meaning.

Daniel told Nebuchadnezzer his dream and its meaning. *"Your Majesty looked, and there before you stood a large statue – an enormous, dazzling statue, awesome in appearance. The head of the statue was made of pure gold, its chest and arms of silver, its belly and thighs of bronze. It had legs of iron. Its feet were partly of iron and partly of baked clay. While you were watching, a rock was cut out, but not by human hands. It struck the statue on its feet of iron and clay and smashed them. Then the iron, the clay, the bronze, the silver and the gold were all broken to pieces and became like chaff on a threshing floor in the summer. The wind swept them away without leaving a trace. But the rock that struck the statue became a huge mountain and filled the whole earth."* (Daniel 2:31-35)

Daniel explained that the head of gold represented Nebuchadnezzar and Babylon. Its chest and its two arms made of silver, represented the kingdom that will come after him, Medo-Persia. –Their King Cyrus would free the Jews from their 70 years of captivity in Babylon and help them return to Jerusalem and to rebuild it, as God promised the prophet Jeremiah as Jerusalem as its people were being killed and carried off to slavery. *"You are saying about this city, 'By the sword, famine and plague it will be given into the hands of the king of Babylon'; but this is what the* LORD, *the God of Israel, says: I will surely gather them from all the lands where*

I banish them in my furious anger and great wrath; I will bring them back to this place and let them live in safety. They will be my people, and I will be their God. I will give them singleness of heart and action, so that they will always fear me and that all will then go well for them and for their children after them. I will make an everlasting covenant with them: I will never stop doing good to them, and I will inspire them to fear me, so that they will never turn away from me. I will rejoice in doing them good and will assuredly plant them in this land with all my heart and soul." (Jeremiah 32:36-42)

Then Daniel continued reciting a list of the greatest kingdoms that will rule the world. After the Persian Empire, there would be a kingdom of bronze (belly and thighs), representing Greece and the worldwide kingdom Alexander the Great created and left to his generals. The legs of iron represent the Roman Empire (both Eastern and Western empires), which came afterwards and crushed the nations of the world. The statue's feet were like the legs, except that the toes are mixed with weak clay. These ten toes represent a revived but weaker Roman Empire, the final great human kingdom that will rise-up during the last 7 years before the Messiah's return. Its capital will be in a city built on 7 hills, Rome.

And then we come to the last kingdom, the Messiah's. He shall replace all worldly governments and establish himself as the world's sole ruler. "*While you were watching, a rock was cut out, but not by human hands. It struck the statue on its feet of iron and clay and smashed them. Then, the iron, the clay, the bronze, the silver, and the gold were all broken to pieces and became like chaff on a threshing floor in the summer. The wind swept them away without leaving a trace. But the rock that struck the statue became a huge mountain and filled the whole earth.* (Daniel 2:30-35)

The King of Babylon

There is an opposing force in God's creation. The bible explains that there was a mighty and beautiful angel called 'Lucifer' in heaven who deceived 1/3 of heaven's angels to join Him in an absurd revolt against God's Son. These are the "dark angels" that affect humanity, the course of our history, and even the destruction of earth's forests, vegetation, and our means of sustenance.

Lucifer is also called "Satan", the "Devil," and in the books of the prophets he is sometimes referred to as the '***King of Babylon.***' (The King of worldliness, deception, and evil.) – Here is a promise to us that this supreme evil creature will be restrained, who the Bible tells us has "***furiously struck down peoples with unceasing blows, angrily beating down nations with relentless persecution.***" (Isaiah 14:6) – No. He will not incite, plague, harm, kill, and destroy any longer. "***In that wonderful day when the Lord gives his people rest from sorrow and fear, from slavery and chains, you will taunt the king of Babylon. You will say, "The mighty man has been destroyed. Yes, your insolence is ended. For the Lord has crushed your wicked power and broken your evil rule. You struck the people with endless blows of rage and held the nations in your angry grip with unrelenting tyranny. But finally, the earth is at rest and quiet. Now it can sing again! Even the trees of the forest– the cypress trees and the cedars of Lebanon sing out this joyous song: 'Since you have been cut down, no one will come now to cut us down!'***" (Isaiah 11:3-8)

The redeemed of the Lord, those who have chosen to change the direction of their lives and to follow in the footsteps of the Messiah, will have the this to say to the devil. "*In that wonderful day when the Lord gives his people rest from sorrow and fear, from slavery and chains, you will jeer at the king of Babylon (Satan) and say, "You bully, you! At last, you have what was coming to you!* ... (Isaiah 14:3-4)

Who Is 'Israel?'

Undeniably, the nation of Israel and their God, Jehovah, have had a very tumultuous relationship. For reasons only known by God's heart, he chose this relatively small race of people to be his special possession. Regardless of their indiscretions, backsliding, rejection, and even the worshipping of other gods, Jehovah has never abandoned them. And he never will. God makes promise after promise about this fact throughout Jewish history. "*But as for you, Israel my servant, Jacob my chosen one, descended from Abraham my friend, I have called you back from the ends of the earth, saying, 'You are my servant.' For I have chosen you and will not throw you away. Don't be afraid, for I am with you. Don't be discouraged, for I am your God. I will strengthen you and help you. I will hold you up with my victorious right hand.*" (Isaiah 41:8-10)

The primary reason for God choosing this particular race He has made very clear, "*I will also make you a light for the Gentiles, that my salvation may reach to the ends of the earth.*" (Isaiah 49:6) Through their prophets, the Maker of all that is seen, and unseen, has revealed his will, his redemption, purpose, and the future He has prepared for this who love Him. – The Messiah accepts everyone who accept Him as their Lord and Savior.

It is very important for you to know that if you are a Believer in the God of Abraham, Isaac, and Jacob then the blessings promised to Israel and the Jews also belong to you. This is explained many times throughout the bible. "*I will bless those who bless you and curse those who treat you with contempt. All the families on earth will be blessed through you.*" (Genesis 12:30)

Everyone who has put their trust in the God of Israel and his Messiah will inherit all that God has prepared for those who love him, Jew, or Non-Jew. So, do not be hesitant nor shy. Know and receive every promise within this book as a promise God has made to you! "*Do not let the son of the foreigner who has joined himself to the Lord speak, saying, "The Lord has utterly separated me from His people… Even to them I will give in my house and within my walls a place and a name better than that of sons and daughters; I will give them an everlasting name that shall not be cut off.*" (Isaiah 56:3,)

"*Even them I will bring to My holy mountain and make them joyful in my house of prayer. Their burnt offerings and their sacrifices will be accepted on my altar; for my house shall be called a house of prayer for all nations.*" The Lord God, who gathers the outcasts of Israel, says, "*Yet I will gather to Him* (the Messiah) *others besides those who are gathered to Him.*" (Isaiah 56:7-8)

Israel, Jerusalem, and the Jewish people become the focus of the entire world just before the Lord's return, according to Scripture. It is in the land of Israel, and in the city of Jerusalem, that the Messiah will reside and from where He will rule the earth. "*Jerusalem will endure through all generations. I will pardon my people's crimes, which I have not yet pardoned; and I, the Lord, will make my home in Jerusalem with my people.*" (Joel 3:20-21)

The prophet Jeremiah was given this message to reassure the Jewish people throughout the ages until his Kingdom comes. "*At that time,*" declares the Lord, "*I will be the God of all the families of Israel, and they will be my people… "I have loved you with an everlasting love; I have drawn you with unfailing kindness. I will build you up again, and you, Virgin Israel, will be rebuilt. Again, you will take up your timbrels and go out to dance with the joyful… For the Lord will deliver Jacob and redeem them from the hand of those stronger than they. They will come and shout for joy on the heights of Zion; they will rejoice in the bounty of the Lord.*" (Jeremiah 31: 1,3-4,11-12)

Throughout history, the Jews have endured slavery, disease, plagues, persecution, imprisonment, and often horrible deaths. The nation of Israel has disappeared multiple times due to a plethora of conquests by much larger and more powerful nations. Repeatedly, their cities have been burned, and their nation left in utter destruction by foreigners. And at times in history, it has been illegal and punishable by death for a Jew to even be found within the borders of Israel. – And yet, for thousands of years, Israel and her people have risen from the ashes to rebuild their nation and their cities again. – For a special people chosen by God to be His "people," it has not been an easy ride. But God has never abandoned them. "*But now, O Jacob, listen to the LORD who created you. O Israel, the one who formed you says, "Do not be afraid, for I have ransomed you. I have called you by name; you are mine.*" (Isaiah 43:1)

As for Jerusalem, it will become the home of the Messiah, from where he will rule and establish a wonderful peace upon the whole world. Of this city, he promises, "*I will rebuild you with precious jewels and make your foundations from lapis lazuli. I will make your towers of sparkling rubies, your gates of shining gems, and your walls of precious stones. I will teach all your children, and they will enjoy great peace. You will be secure under a government that is just and fair.*" (Isaiah 54:11-14)

His Temple and his throne will be there. – The prophet Ezekiel is given a detailed description and measurement of the New Jerusalem that the Messiah shall build. "*Then the Spirit took me up and brought me into the inner courtyard, and the glory of the LORD filled the Temple. And I heard someone speaking to me from within the Temple, while the man who had been measuring stood beside me. The LORD said to me, "Son of man, this is the place of my throne and the place where I will rest my feet. I will live here forever among the people of Israel.*" (Ezekiel 43:5–7)

Jews are special because God spoke to Abraham and Moses and established the Jewish people as a nation in Israel and Judah. They follow religious practices and holy days and festivals throughout each year, commemorating God's historical interventions and miracles that he has performed for them. And they seek to abide by the laws that were given to them by God through Moses. -- But currently, very few have a belief nor expectation that the Messiah is real. – This prevalent attitude of disbelief has plagued the Jews since Moses tried to take them to the 'Promised Land.' Many of the Old Testament prophecies reveal the frustration that God has had in keeping Jews faithful to Him. However, there has always remained a remanent of faithful believers. Indeed, much of the Bible's prophecies refer to a worldwide revival of faith among the Jews in the 'last days.' *"For the LORD will deliver Jacob and redeem Israel...They will come and shout for joy on the heights of Zion; they will rejoice in the bounty of the LORD."* (Jeremiah 31:11–14)

"This is the covenant I will make with the people of Israel after that time," declares the LORD. *"I will put my law in their minds and write it on their hearts. I will be their God, and they will be my people...They will all know me, from the least of them to the greatest,"* declares the LORD. *"For I will forgive their wickedness and will remember their sins no more."* (Jeremiah 31:33–37)

There is an evil that has plagued humanity since the Abraham. It is hatred toward the Jews. I warn you to avoid such thoughts or involvement, in any way. *"The Lord said to Abram . . . "I will make of you a great nation, and I will bless you and make your name great, so that you will be a blessing. I will bless those who bless you, and him who dishonors you I will curse, and in you all the families of the earth shall be blessed."* (Genesis 12:1–3)

God has not forgotten his beloved chosen people, the children of Abraham. He will bring them back to Him. In our times ahead, we will see this happen in this generation. *"Brothers and sisters, here is a mystery I want you to understand. It will keep you from being proud. Part of Israel has refused to obey God. That will continue until the full number of Gentiles has entered God's kingdom. In this way all Israel will be saved. It is written, "The God who saves will come from Mount Zion. He will remove sin from Jacob's family. Here is my covenant with them. I will take away their sins." -- As far as the good news is concerned, the people of Israel are enemies. This is for your good. But as far as God's choice is concerned, the people of Israel are loved. This is because of God's promises to the founders of that nation. God does not take back his gifts. He does not change his mind about those he has chosen."* (Romans 11:25–30)

New Testament Prophecy

In the Jewish language, the word for 'Messiah' is *'Mashiach,'* which means *'the chosen one.'* In Greek, the original language of the New Testament, the word is *'Christos.* Its meaning is *'the one chosen to deliver.'* – Hence, all Believers in the 'Christos' wait with expectancy the coming of heaven's divine Deliverer to come to earth and rescue our world at the end of this age. And the purpose of this book is to encourage and excite you about this new world and its righteous and loving King who is coming!

Between the last book of the Old Testament and the first book of New Testament there is a period of over 400 years without Israel having a prophet. Those years were extremely tumultuous. Israel was invaded by multiple stronger nations that used that land primarily as a battle ground. The Greeks, Egyptians, and Romans all had great wars there. Finally, Rome conquered those nations and enforced peace in Israel by military might. – It was then, that a unique birth occurred that the Old Testament prophets had all promised, the birth of God's Son, the Messiah.

"Therefore, the Lord himself will give you a sign: The virgin will conceive and give birth to a son and will call him 'Immanuel' (God with us.)." (Isaiah 7:14) From out of all the glorious references throughout the Old Testament about the coming reign of the Messiah, this promise, given to the righteous king Hezekiah, tells us about the birth of the 'Son of God.' He will issue forth from a "***virgin***" and his name will mean "God with us."

The New Testament begins with the Book of Matthew, a Jew living in Israel during the Roman occupation. Jesus chose him to become a disciple and an Apostle. -- Matthew refers to this prophecy, and the advent of the Messiah in his first chapter, "*Now the birth of Jesus Christ took place in this way. When his mother Mary had been betrothed to Joseph, before they came together, she was found to be with child from the Holy Spirit.*" (Matthew 1:18) Her betrothed, Joseph, was naturally dismayed and very confused. And then a messenger from heaven appeared to him, "*But as he considered these things, behold, an angel of the Lord appeared to him in a dream, saying, "Joseph, son of David, do not fear to take Mary as your wife, for that which is conceived in her is from the Holy Spirit. She will bear a son, and you shall call his name Jesus, for he will save his people from their sins.*" (Matthew 1:20-21) – (The name Jesus is derived from the Hebrew name 'Yeshua,' meaning 'to deliver or to rescue.')

Jesus was not born like most kings. His parents were not wealthy and living in a palace. No. He was born humbly, in a barn surrounded by animals, with their hay as his bed, in the small town of Bethlehem. This was promised by the prophet Micah. "*But you, Bethlehem Ephrathah, who are small among the clans of Judah, out of you will come forth for Me One to be ruler over Israel--One whose origins are of old, from the days of eternity.*" (Micah 5:2)

Another disciple and Apostle, Luke, a physician, gives this account. -- There were shepherds tending their sheep that night on the hillsides of Bethlehem. "*Suddenly, an angel of the Lord appeared among them, and the radiance of the Lord's glory surrounded them. They were terrified, but the angel reassured them. "Don't be afraid!" he said. "I bring you good news that will bring great joy to all people. The Savior—yes, the Messiah, the Lord—has been born today in Bethlehem.*" (Luke 2:9-11) That angel was joined by a host of more angels, singing. "*Glory to God in highest heaven, and peace on earth to those with whom God is pleased.*" (Luke 2:14)

We are also told that Jesus' father was carpenter. No doubt, Jesus helped him with his work as grew up. He also had younger sisters and 3 younger brothers to help his mother raise. He grew up like most other boys, while also being fully aware of who he was and the purpose of his life. – When he was 12, his parents took him to a huge, multi-day festival in Jerusalem. He became separated from his parents, and they took 3 days before finding him. *"He was found in The Temple in discussion with the elders. They were amazed at his learning, especially given his young age. When admonished by Mary, Jesus replied: "How is it that you sought me? Did you not know that I must be in my Father's house?"* (Matthew 2:6)

When Jesus was 30, he began publicly proclaiming that he was the Messiah. He proved it by doing miracles, feeding the hungry, and healing them of all infirmities. *"The people were amazed when they saw the mute speaking, the crippled made well, the lame walking and the blind seeing. And they praised the God of Israel."* (Matthew 15:31)

But the ultimate purpose of His first advent was to become the Passover Lamb of God, and to cleanse mankind of the guilt of sin, once and for all! *"From that time on, Jesus began to explain to his disciples that he must go to Jerusalem and suffer many things at the hands of the elders, the chief priests and the teachers of the law, and that he must be killed, and on the third day be raised to life."* (Matthew 16:21)

Jesus instructed his disciples and followers how they should live if they truly have decided to love God and to obey His laws. And this is the key He shared with us to accomplishing that. *"You have heard that it was said, 'Love your neighbor and hate your enemy.' But I tell you, love your enemies and pray for those who persecute you, that you may be children of your Father in heaven. He causes his sun to rise on the evil and the good and sends rain on the righteous and the unrighteous. If you love those who love you, what reward will you get? Are not even the tax collectors* (sinners) *doing that? And if you greet only your own people, what are you doing more than others? Do not even pagans* (unbelievers) *do that? Be perfect, therefore, as your heavenly Father is perfect."* (Matthew 5:43-48)

The most telling proof of one having a true faith in God, and the coming of His Messiah to rescue and heal our world, is the development of LOVE for ALL within your heart and soul. *"Plant the good seeds of righteousness, and you will harvest a crop of love. Plow up the hard ground of your hearts, for now is the time to seek the LORD, that he may come and shower righteousness upon you."* (Hosea 10:12) – It is not by our labor and good deeds that we are saved. We receive eternal life when we choose to allow our lives to be transformed by the indwelling of God's Holy Spirit. And the proof of that is the love of God for others which possesses us. *"So then, by their fruit you will recognize them. Not everyone who says to Me, "Lord, Lord, will enter the kingdom of heaven, but only those who do the will of my Father in heaven."* (Matthew 7:21)

Jesus is not coming to rescue 'good' and 'perfect' people. He is coming to save those who know that they have fallen short of God's high calling, the humble and contrite. *"For I have not come to call the righteous, but sinners."* (Matthew 9:13) In fact, it is in confessing our failures and sins that we are saved, not by ignoring that we have no faults.

The idea that in these fleshly bodies, with their craving and needs, that we shall someday be completely free from conflicting desires that war against our higher aspirations, is not possible. This battle shall continue until we are freed from this temporal body and receive perfect, eternal bodies. – We all do things that we know that we should not. It is the human condition. However, when one commits themselves to seeking after the Lord and doing all that He asks to the best of our abilities, the Lord gives them a Helper, the "Holy Spirit."

"If you love me, keep my commands. And I will ask the Father, and he will give you another advocate to help you and be with you forever— the Spirit of truth. God is Spirit, and they who worship Him must worship in spirit and in truth." (John 14:15-17) God is also a person. He has a body that dwells in such intense light and power that no human being can survive in His presence. *"He alone can never die, and he lives in light so brilliant that no*

human can approach him. No human eye has ever seen him, nor ever will. All honor and power to him forever! Amen." (1st Timothy 6:16) God is both a distinct person that someday in our new bodies we can be with forever. He is also a Spirit that can be everywhere, with everyone, at the same time. And then there is God's Son, who has become one of us, a human, who fully understands our struggles and weaknesses. "*The Word became flesh and made his dwelling among us. We have seen his glory, the glory of the one and only Son, who came from the Father, full of grace and truth.*" (John 1:14)

The intimate connection between the 'Father' and the 'Messiah' is sometimes indistinguishable. So much so that when Jesus was asked by his disciples to "show them the Father," he replied, "*Don't you know me, even after I have been among you such a long time? Anyone who has seen me has seen the Father. How can you say, 'Show us the Father'?*" (John 14:9) – We also read this in the Old Testament, when we are told the Messiah's name when he reigns on earth. It shall be, "*Wonderful Counselor, Mighty God, Everlasting Father, Prince of Peace.*" (Isaiah 9:6)

Jesus further explains his union with the Father to his disciples, "*Believe that I am in the Father, and that the Father is in me. The words I say to you I do not speak on my own authority. Rather, it is the Father, living in me, who is doing his work. Believe me when I say that I am in the Father and the Father is in me; or at least believe on the evidence of the works themselves.*" (John 14:10-11)

Of course, this union is mysterious to us. But we are told that when the Messiah returns, "*On that day you will realize that I am in my Father, and you are in me, and I am in you.*" (John 14:20) Someday, we will come to know God as we are known by Him.

In the last book of the bible a scene in heaven is described as the Messiah begins His reign "*I heard what sounded like the roar of a great multitude in heaven shouting "Hallelujah! Salvation and glory and power belong to our God… "Hallelujah! For our Lord God Almighty reigns. Let us rejoice and be glad and give him glory!*" (Revelation 19:6-7)

And here is another revelation as to what will happen at the end of this age when the Christ establishes his Kingdom on earth. "*Then I saw "a new heaven and a new earth," for the first heaven and the first earth had passed away, and there was no longer any sea. I saw the Holy City, the new Jerusalem, coming down out of heaven from God, prepared as a bride beautifully dressed for her husband. And I heard a loud voice from the throne saying, "Look! God's dwelling place is now among the people, and he will dwell with them. They will be his people, and God himself will be with them and be their God. 'He will wipe every tear from their eyes. There will be no more death' or mourning or crying or pain, for the old order of things has passed away.*" (Revelation 21:1-4)

Our God wants us to know these things! This is the wisdom that will provide strength and hope and endurance through any hardship. He does not want us to be afraid, but to be stalwart and steady in our confidence in Him and His Kingdom to come. "*He who was seated on the throne said, "I am making everything new!" Then he said, "Write this down, for these words are trustworthy and true.*" (Revelation 21: 5)

The Bible closes with these words of encouragement for we who live during our time, "*Look, I am coming soon! My reward is with me, and I will give to each person according to what they have done. I am the Alpha and the Omega, the First and the Last, the Beginning and the End.*" (Revelation 22:12)

Salvation

We all must take stock of ourselves and examine our walk with God. If there are any lingering sins that continue to afflict us, then seek repentance even more earnestly. At the very least, confess it to the Lord, and if possible, to another trusted Believer who will pray with you. Also, dive deeply into God's word. Read it everyday without fail. It will strengthen your faith and enable you to overcome all obstacles. And find fellowship with other believers who are focused on the Lord and His return. *"Do this, knowing the time, that it is already the hour for you to awaken from sleep; for now, salvation is nearer to us than when we first believed."* (Romans 13:11)

The Messiah himself gave us this warning to be sure of our steady walk with Him, and to be ready for the day that he returns, *"However, no one knows the day or hour when these things will happen, not even the angels in heaven or the Son himself. Only the Father knows. And since you don't know when that time will come, be on guard! Stay alert!"* (Mark 13:32-33) – In these final days before the Son of God returns to cleanse this earth of evil and those who practice such things, it is imperative that we live as if Jesus was returning today!

Now is not the time for us to slip away from following the ways of God. Be steadfast, patient, and persevere. *"Son of man, give your people this message: The righteous behavior of righteous people will not save them if they turn to sin, nor will the wicked behavior of wicked people destroy them if they repent and turn from their sins."* (Ezekiel 33:12)

Do not be afraid. The Lord will never reject anyone who calls to Him for help and redemption. It is not His desire to judge and punish us for our selfish and sinful ways. *"Comfort, comfort my people," says your God. "Speak tenderly (to them). Tell her that her sad days are gone, and her sins are pardoned."* (Isaiah 40:1-2)

If we call to our Maker in sincerity of our hearts, confess our sins, and ask for forgiveness, it shall be given! *"Everyone who calls on the name of the LORD will be saved."* (Joel 2:12)

Everyone who has chosen to believe in God and His Messiah, Jesus the Christ, were known by the Lord before the worlds began. *"You have been chosen to know me, believe in me, and understand that I alone am God. There is no other God—there never has been, and there never will be. I, yes, I, am the LORD, and there is no other Savior."* (Isaiah 43:10-11)

When God forgives, He also forgets. And it should be the same for us with others too. *"I—yes, I alone—will blot out your sins for my own sake and will never think of them again."* (Isaiah 43:25)

"I have swept away your sins like a cloud. I have scattered your offenses like the morning mist. Oh, return to me, for I have paid the price to set you free." (Isaiah 44:22)

Indeed! There is no other God but the God of the Bible! *"For there is no other God but me, a righteous God and Savior. There is none but me. Let all the world look to me for salvation! For I am God; there is no other. Every knee will bend to me, and every tongue will declare allegiance to me." The people will declare, "The LORD is the source of all my righteousness and strength."* (Isaiah 45:21-24)

The wounds that Jesus received when nailed to His cross will never disappear. Those wounds are an eternal proof of God's overwhelming desire to love us, and to have an intimate, loving relationship with us forever. *"Can a mother forget the baby at her breast and have no compassion on the child she has borne? Though she may forget, I will not forget you! See, I have engraved you on the palms of my hands."* (Isaiah 49:15-16)

"Come to me with your ears wide open. Listen, and you will find life. I will make an everlasting covenant with you. I will give you all my unfailing love." (Isaiah 55:3)

If you have not yet ever spoken to Jesus and asked Him for forgiveness and to be given a new spirit, His Holy Spirit, within you, then turn to Him right now and ask. *"Seek the Lord while you can find him. Call on him now while he is near. Let the wicked change their ways and banish the very thought of doing wrong. Let them turn to the Lord that he may have mercy on them. Yes, turn to our God, for he will forgive generously."* (Isaiah 56:6-7)

Jesus does not expect us to be sinless and perfect before we come to Him. He wants us as we are now. *"For I have not come to call the righteous, but sinners."* (Matthew 9:13) As we dedicate our lives to pleasing Him, we are changed more and more into His image. *"Your Teacher will no longer hide Himself—with your own eyes you will see Him. And whether you turn to the right or to the left, your ears will hear this command behind you: "This is the Way. Walk in it!"* (Isaiah 30:21)

Jesus says that the indwelling of His Holy Spirit is like the planting of a seed. Overtime, as we choose to walk with Jesus everyday, and to follow in His footsteps, we are changed. *"He told them another parable: "The kingdom of heaven is like a mustard seed, which a man took and planted in his field. Though it is the smallest of all seeds, yet when it grows, it is the largest of garden plants and becomes a tree, so that the birds come and perch in its branches."* (Matthew 13:31-32) Regardless of how insignificant and powerless we may be now, when we grow in the Lord, we are transformed. He uses our life to bless the lives of others.

Only when we see God as our loving Creator who desires to forgive and to restore us, can we trust Him. He is not our enemy seeking to judge us. No. Our Maker loves us far more than we can know. *"However, God is rich in mercy. He brought us to life with Christ while we were dead as a result of those things that we did wrong. He did this because of the great love that he has for us. You are saved by God's grace!"* (Ephesians 2:4-5) – *"The Lord is... longsuffering to us-ward, not willing that any should perish, but that all should come to repentance."* (2 Peter 3:9)

If you have asked Jesus to forgive you, accept you, and help you, then the Spirit of God resides within you. The Bible teaches us that the Holy Spirit helps to direct our paths and lead us in the ways of righteousness. Ask to be delivered from those sins that have plagued us and that we have been unable to overcome. *"I am the vine; you are the branches. If you remain in me and I in you, you will bear much fruit; apart from me you can do nothing. If you do not remain in me, you are like a branch that is thrown away and withers; such branches are picked up, thrown into the fire and burned. If you remain in me and my words remain in you, ask whatever you wish, and it will be done for you. This is to my Father's glory, that you bear much fruit, showing yourselves to be my disciples."* (John 15:5-8)

As human beings, we are unable to walk in holiness. There are too many things in this world that concern us. We are always worrying about our sustenance and survival. Our anxieties consist of trying to provide for ourselves and our loved ones. It is not the Lord's will for us to do this. *"So, don't worry about these things, saying, 'What will we eat? What will we drink? What will we wear?' These things dominate the thoughts of unbelievers, but your heavenly Father already knows all your needs. Seek the Kingdom of God above all else, and live righteously, and he will give you everything you need."* (Matthew 6:25-33)

There is no lasting peace in this world. Everything is subject to change. Christ gives us a peace that is transcendent of this world and its worries. The assurance that He is always with us is our strength. We are never alone. *"Peace I leave with you; my peace I give you. I do not give to you as the world gives. Do not let your hearts be troubled and do not be afraid." "I am leaving you with a gift—peace of mind and heart."* (John 14:27)

Place your faith in God and see how your anxious thoughts dissipate. *"Happy are those who trust in the Lord, who rely on the Lord."* (Jeremiah 17:7)

Faith

"Now faith is confidence in what we hope for and the assurance of what we do not see."

~ Hebrews 11:1 ~

The essential step to receiving eternal life is enduring **Faith**. Here is a story Jesus told that explains the difference between true, lasting faith, and false faith. – Jesus told a story of a farmer going out into his field and scattering seeds to grow a harvest. He compares this to how different people receive God's plan to save us, as seeds landing on different kinds of soil. "***When anyone hears the message about the kingdom and does not understand it, the evil one comes and snatches away what was sown in their heart. This is the seed sown along the path. --The seed falling on rocky ground refers to someone who hears the word and at once receives it with joy. But since they have no root, they last only a short time. When trouble or persecution comes because of the word, they quickly fall away. --The seed falling among the thorns refers to someone who hears the word, but the worries of this life and the deceitfulness of wealth choke the word, making it unfruitful. --But the seed falling on good soil refers to someone who hears the word and understands it. This is the one who produces a crop, yielding a hundred, sixty or thirty times what was sown.***" (Matthew 13:19-23)

Living a consistent life that pleases the Lord is a lifetime process that is not completed until we see Him face to face. Our test in this life is to persevere and to endure. Sometimes we find ourselves out of money, out of strength, out of ideas, out of opportunities, or alone and without anyone who cares. But the Believer is never out of everything, for we always have God. And with God, we have everything. That fact alone is enough to motivate us to worship Him and wait for His answers.

That's what King Jehoshaphat of Judah did when his nation was surrounded by three neighboring armies. Judah was far outnumbered. Jehoshaphat prayed a lengthy prayer of praise, concluding with these words: *"Nor do we know what to do, but our eyes are upon You"* (2 Chronicles 20:12). All they had was their faith in God's providence. So, a prophet directed the king to set out for battle, praising and worshiping the Lord as they went. And God routed the enemy armies and delivered Judah. God was all they had, and in the middle of worshiping Him, they were delivered. – There are no obstacles that cannot be overcome with God on our side.

If you are at the end of your resources today, if you don't know what to do, turn your eyes toward God and wait for His deliverance. "*Come to me, all you who are weary and burdened, and I will give you rest. Take my yoke upon you and learn from me, for I am gentle and humble in heart, and you will find rest for your souls. For my yoke is easy and my burden is light.*" (Matthew 11:28-30)

As the time of the Lord's coming draws nigh, times will become increasingly difficult. "*Because of the multiplication of wickedness, the love of most will grow cold. But the one who perseveres to the end will be saved.*" (Matthew 24:12-13)

Hear the wisdom given to King David for our benefit and peace. "*Do not fret because of those who are evil or be envious of those who do wrong; for like the grass they will soon wither, like green plants they will soon die away. Trust in the LORD and do good; dwell in the land and enjoy safe pasture. Take delight in the LORD, and he will give you the desires of your heart. Commit your way to the* Lord; *trust in him and he will do this: He will make your righteous reward shine like the dawn, your vindication like the noonday sun.*" (Psalm 37:1-6)

Learning to trust God by faith is a learning process. We grow in faith as we continue to seek after the Lord. Just know that FAITH is all that matters. True faith is truly transformative. It is also essential. "*And without faith it is impossible to please him, for whoever would draw near to God must believe that he exists and that he rewards those who seek him.*" (Hebrews 11:6)

Our Savior promises to greatly reward those who put their faith and trust in Him. "*He who has an ear, let him hear what the Spirit says to the churches* (Believers). *To him who overcomes, I will give to eat of the Tree of Life, which in the Paradise of God.*" (Revelation 2:7) This tree is symbolic of eternal life.

Repentance

Once one believes in the wonderful love and forgiveness of God, and sincerely receives the grace we are offered, it will result in repentance. – We might have tried to live a perfect life, but those efforts always fail. Because without believing in and receiving God's love it is impossible. "*Don't you realise that God's kindness is meant to lead you to repentance?*" (Romans 2:4) It is God's love that must draw us to Him. As we continue to grow in our realization of how immense and infinite that love is, our natural response is to love Him in return. And that results in our changing our behavior so that what we do always pleases Him.

"*Then Jesus said to his disciples, "Whoever wants to be my disciple must deny themselves and take up their cross and follow me. For whoever wants to save their life will lose it, but whoever loses their life for me will find it… For the Son of Man is going to come in his Father's glory with his angels, and then he will reward each person according to what they have done.*" (Matthew 16:27) The human condition is such that even when we choose to do good, other wants and needs within us often fight against our better desires as we seek to follow in God's ways. In fact, the bible teaches that trying to be godly by human will is impossible. "*So, I say, walk by the Spirit, and you will not gratify the desires of the flesh. For the flesh craves what is contrary to the Spirit, and the Spirit what is contrary to the flesh. They are opposed to each other, so that you do not do what you want. But if you are led by the Spirit, you are not under the law.*" (Galatians 5:16-18)

Those who live by trying to be good will fail. It is only by understanding and relying on the immensity of God's love for us and his overwhelming desire to bless us forever as his eternal children that we can behave like the people of God. Focusing on obedience is futile. Focus instead on LOVE. Receive God's love for you and share that love, lovingly, with others. – This will result in obedience and salvation.

Now, be warned. Until these temporal fleshly bodies are replaced with our promised eternal bodies, sin will still lurk within us. We will still sometimes sin and do things that we know God does not want us to do. But because we are God's children, there is a remedy when we do slip back into our fleshly desires. *"If we claim to be without sin, we deceive ourselves and the truth is not in us. If we confess our sins, he is faithful and just and will forgive us our sins and purify us from all unrighteousness."* (John 1:8-9) – Do not hide from our loving Savior when we fail. Confess your sins, and in sincerity let God know you are sorry. Then get back up immediately and continue following in Christ's footsteps.

This is why we are given God's Holy Spirit when we decide to give our lives to Christ. We are given the power to transform! *"But the fruit of the Spirit is love, joy, peace, patience, kindness, goodness, faithfulness, gentleness, and self-control. Against such things there is no law."* (Galatians 5:22-23) Just as Jesus was able to willingly go to his cross and be crucified in order to free mankind from judgement and sin through God's power, we are also given this power to control our actions and emotions. – Once we become Believers in Jesus the Messiah, it becomes our goal to 'walk in the Spirit.' *"Those who belong to Christ Jesus have crucified the flesh with its passions and desires. Since we live by the Spirit, let us walk in step with the Spirit."* (Galatians 5:16-23)

Once we have committed our lives to the Lord in faith, we have nothing more to fear. *"The LORD is compassionate and gracious, slow to anger, abounding in love. He will not always accuse, nor will he harbor his anger forever; he does not treat us as our sins deserve or repay us accord-*

ing to our iniquities. For as high as the heavens are above the earth, so great is his love for those who fear him; as far as the east is from the west, so far has he removed our transgressions from us." (Psalm 103:8-12)

As we grow in faith and the assurance of God's love for us, quitting the things we once did, brings a sense of closeness and intimacy with God. "*This is what the Sovereign Lord says, "In repentance and rest is your salvation, in quietness and trust is your strength.*" (Isaiah 30:15)

"*Repent, then, and turn to God, so that your sins may be wiped out, that times of refreshing may come from the Lord, and that he may send the Messiah, who has been appointed for you—even Jesus.*" (Acts 3:19-20)

"*Do this, knowing the time, that it is already the hour for you to awaken from sleep; for now salvation is nearer to us than when we believed.*" (Romans 13:11)

And lastly, heed this warning from our Savior, "*Therefore be on the alert, for you do not know which day your Lord is coming.*" (Matthew 24:42)

Baptism

Some of the final words that Jesus spoke to his disciples were this, "*Go therefore and make disciples of all nations, baptizing them in the name of the Father and of the Son and of the Holy Spirit, teaching them to observe all that I have commanded you. And behold, I am with you always, to the end of the age.*" (Matthew 28:18-20).

Believers in Jesus the Messiah are baptised in water after asking Him to save them from their sins. We do so because Jesus asked us to do so. This is ceremonial and practical. – As we lay backwards into the water, it is like being buried in a grave along with our old ways of living. And when we rise out of the water, it is like being raised from the dead to live a new life! – We also are baptised because that is when we receive God's Holy Spirit into our heart and soul. "*He will baptize you with the Holy Spirit and fire.*" (Matthew 3:11)

We are also baptised for the practical purpose of giving us the strength and motivation to share this fantastic news with the world. "*But you will receive power when the Holy Spirit has come upon you, and you will be my witnesses in Jerusalem and in all Judea and Samaria, and to the end of the earth.*" (Acts 1:8) The "*power*" that Jesus mentions comes from the Greek work '*dunamis*,' which means 'power, potential, and ability.' It is also from where we get the word 'dynamite.'

The Holy Spirit leads us in the Paths of Righteousness. He whispers in our hearts and tells us the will of God. He shows what is truth and what is error. He is the proof of our adoption as God's children. "*But the Advocate, the Holy Spirit, whom the Father will send in my name, will teach you all things and will remind you of everything I have said to you.*" (John 14:26)

The Holy Spirit gives us the desire to do God's will. He is the source of our faith and gives us the strength and the power we need to persevere in seeking holiness, peace, and the love of God, regardless of our circumstances. "*May the God of hope fill you with all joy and peace as you trust in him, so that you may overflow with hope by the power of the Holy Spirit.*" (Romans 15:13)

"*Repent and be baptised every one of you in the name of Jesus Christ for the forgiveness of your sins, and you will receive the gift of the Holy Spirit.*" (Acts 2:38)

Baptism joins us to the worldwide body of Believers. We may have divergent of views about many things, but we are always to maintain the unity of our mutual faith in God's Son, our Savior. "*For by one Spirit are we all baptized into one body, whether we be Jews or Gentiles, whether we be bond or free; and have been all made to drink into one Spirit.*" (1 Corinthians 12:13)

Above all, do not judge, but forgive and love everyone, not just Believers. "*A new commandment I give to you, that you love one another: just as I have loved you, you also are to love one another. By this all people will know that you are my disciples, if you have love for one another.*" – Jesus (1 John 13:34-35)

The End Times

"With this news, strengthen those who have tired hands, and encourage those who have weak knees. Say to those with fearful hearts, "Be strong, and do not fear, for your God is coming to destroy your enemies. He is coming to save you."

~ Isaiah 35:3-4 ~

When the Apostles were with Jesus, they asked several times about the "End Times" and what the signs of His coming again will be. There are also many verses from the Old Testament about this time too. In short, there will be hard times ahead before His return. But the glory that awaits us afterwards is so tremendous that it is our Light in the midst of these few years of darkness ahead.

However, there is this promise! *"**Because you have obeyed my command to persevere, I will protect you from the great time of testing that will come upon the whole world to test those who belong to this world**."* (Revelation 3:10)– This wonderful promise is given to those who belong to the Church of Philadelphia (Brotherly Love). – Jesus encouraged these Believers to continue in their loving faith for Him and for others, and to hold on and wait patiently until his coming. By doing so, they will be protected from the tribulations of the last years on earth before his return.

Whatever awaits us, promises such as this should vitalize our endurance. "*I am coming soon. Hold on to what you have, so that no one will take your crown. The one who is victorious I will make a pillar in the temple of my God. Never again will they leave it. I will write on them the name of my God and the name of the city of my God, the new Jerusalem, which is coming down out of heaven from my God; and I will also write on them my new name. Whoever has ears, let them hear.*" (Revelation 3:11-13)

You may ask, "How would Jesus '*protect*' us from the "great time of testing?" – That is a wonderful question, and it is my thrill to tell you.

You may have heard Believers mention the "Rapture." This word means to be "caught -up." It refers to this promise: "*Behold! I tell you a mystery. We shall not all sleep* (die), *but we shall all be changed, in a moment, in the twinkling of an eye, at the last trumpet. For the trumpet will sound, and the dead will be raised imperishable, and we shall be changed. For this perishable body must put on the imperishable, and this mortal body must put on immortality. When the perishable puts on the imperishable, and the mortal puts on immortality, then shall come to pass the saying that is written: "Death is swallowed up in victory. O' death, where is your victory? O' death, where is your sting?*" (1 Corinthians 15:51-58) – Before Jesus comes back to save and heal our world, everyone who belongs to Him will be raised and given a new, perfect, eternal body!

Not all Believers will taste death. We who are still alive, will have our bodies and minds transformed in an instant while still living! "*Let not your hearts be troubled; believe in God, believe also in Me. In my Father's house are many rooms; if it were not so, would I have told you that I go to prepare a place for you? And when I go and prepare a place for you, I will come again and will take you to myself, that where I am you may be also.*" (John 14:1-3)

Jesus also gave us this comforting assurance, "*For this is the will of My Father, that everyone who beholds the Son and believes in Him, may have eternal life; and I Myself will raise him up on the last day.*" (John 6:40)

The Tribulation

I hesitate to mention this. My intent for this book is not to frighten anyone. Just the opposite! But to be complete, I must say a few difficult things. We are told throughout the Bible that there will be a period of judgement upon the earth just prior to our Lord's return. This time is referred to as the "time of tribulation.' It will last for a period of 7 years, and then the Lord will descend from heaven to end the suffering, to restore the earth, and to establish His everlasting Kingdom. – Jesus warns us that… *"For then there will be great distress, unequaled from the beginning of the world until now—and never to be equaled again. If those days had not been cut short, no one would survive, but for the sake of the elect those days will be shortened."* (Matthew 24:21-22) We and our loved ones do not have to experience the final years of trial that is coming. We all can be rescued from that time if we are faithful and full of God's love for others.

One day as Jesus and his disciples were walking near the Temple in Jerusalem, his disciples mentioned to Jesus how beautiful the Temple was. In reply, the Lord told them that the Temple would one day be destroyed. *"Truly I tell you, not one stone here will be left on another; every one will be thrown down."* (Matthew 24:2) (And indeed, not long after Jesus' crucifixion, the Romans crushed a Jewish revolt, burned the city, and tore down the temple in 70 A.D., just as Jesus had said.) – Then the disciples asked, *"Tell us,' They said, 'When will this happen, and what will be the sign of your coming and of the end of the age?"* (Matthew 24:3)

Jesus answered that question and gave them, and we who are living just prior to the Lord's return, critical things to look for. His first response was a warning about false prophets. *"Jesus answered: "Watch out that no one deceives you. For many will come in my name, claiming, 'I am the Messiah,' and will deceive many... At that time many will turn away from the faith and will betray and hate each other, and many false prophets will appear and deceive many people. Because of the increase of wickedness, the love of most will grow cold, but the one who stands firm to the end will be saved."* (Matthew 24:5,10-13)

Here is a summary of the details of what Jesus told his disciples to watch and look for as signs of his imminent return in Matthew 24:

1. Deception by false teachers. *"For many will come in my name, claiming, 'I am the Messiah,' and will deceive many."* (Verse 5)

2. Dissension among nations. *"You will hear of wars and rumors of wars; but see to it that you are not alarmed. Such things must happen, but the end is still to come. Nation will rise against nation, and kingdom against kingdom."* (Verses 6-7)

3. Devastation disease, and disasters worldwide. *"There will be famines and earthquakes in various places."* (Verse 7)

4. Martyrdom of Believers: *"Then you will be handed over to be persecuted and put to death, and you will be hated by all nations because of me."* (Verse 9)

5. Betrayal by friends and family. *"At that time many will turn away from the faith and will betray and hate each other."* (Verse 10)

6. Rampant lawlessness and hatred. *"Because of the increase of wickedness, the love of most will grow cold."* (Verse 12)

Hopefully, those Believers who were not ready for the Lord's return, who knew the truth, but put off acting on it, will repent. Then they and those who will come to believe during these 7 years are assured, *"but the one who stands firm to the end will be saved."* It is those who will be sharing about the Jesus and his Kingdom to come during this time. "*And this gospel of the kingdom will be preached in the whole world as a testimony to all nations, and then the end will come.*" (Verse 14)

As we have seen, there are many prophecies throughout the Bible about this time, just before Christ comes. Jesus alludes to a prophecy given in the book of Daniel to further explain the time of his coming to his disciples. It describes the Anti-Christ, the most powerful ruler on earth at that time, erecting a statue of himself within Jerusalem's Temple. Jesus gives these instructions to Believers when it happens, "*So when you see standing in the holy place 'the abomination that causes desolation,' spoken of through the prophet Daniel—let the reader understand —then let those who are in Judea flee to the mountains.*" (Matthew 24:15-16) He tells them to "*flee*" because everyone who fails to bow down and worship this statue of the Anti-Christ will be killed. (Other scripture tells us where these believers in Jerusalem will hide. It will be in the land surrounding the ancient and abandoned city of Petra in Jordan.) There they will be cared for and fed until the Lord descends from heaven and his feet touch the Mount of Olives. "*On that day his feet will stand on the Mount of Olives, east of Jerusalem, and the Mount of Olives will be split in two from east to west, forming a great valley... Then the* L̲ᴏʀᴅ *my God will come, and all the holy ones with him... On that day living water will flow out from Jerusalem, half of it east to the Dead Sea and half of it west to the Mediterranean Sea, in summer and in winter. The* L̲ᴏʀᴅ *will be king over the whole earth. On that day there will be one* L̲ᴏʀᴅ, *and his name the only name.*" (Zechariah 14:1-9)

The Lord's return for Believers will be the most wonderful and glorious day on earth. He will heal and replenish our world and make it more lush and more beautiful than ever before. He will rule the nations and maintain law and order and establish peace across the whole earth. His reign will be for everlasting.

But for those who refuse to heed the call of God to believe, repent, and obey there will be judgement. "*For see, the day of the Lord is com-*

ing, the terrible day of his wrath and fierce anger. The land shall be destroyed and all the sinners with it. The heavens will be black above them. No light will shine from stars or sun or moon. And I will punish the world for its evil, the wicked for their sin; I will crush the arrogance of the proud man and the haughtiness of the rich. Few will live when I have finished up my work. Men will be as scarce as gold—of greater value than the gold of Ophir. For I will shake the heavens in my wrath and fierce anger, and the earth will move from its place in the skies." (Isaiah 13: 9-13)

The Tribulation is not for those of us who have turned away from living for ourselves and dedicated our lives to serving the Lord. We will be saved from this time. But those who hesitate, or resist, must endure it. Be prudent and wise! Avoid this judgement that is coming, "*I will sweep away everything from the face of the earth,*" says the LORD. "*I will sweep away people and animals alike. I will sweep away the birds of the sky and the fish in the sea. I will reduce the wicked to heaps of rubble, and I will wipe humanity from the face of the earth,*" says the LORD." (Zephaniah 1:2-3)

Accept the free gift of forgiveness and salvation offered by Jesus Christ now! He has already received the judgement due to us. "***Before the decree takes effect and that day passes like windblown chaff, before the LORD's fierce anger comes upon you, before the day of the LORD's wrath comes upon you. Seek the LORD, all you humble of the land, you who do what he commands. Seek righteousness, seek humility; perhaps you will be sheltered on the day of the LORD's anger.***" (Zephaniah 2:2-3) The proud and arrogant people who abuse others and fail to heed God's law to love others, will be no more.

However, true believers in the Messiah, who have kept their hearts lit with the Spirit of God, and kept their faith through trials and persecution, will enter into an eternity of bliss, beauty, love, and righteousness. "***But I will leave within you the meek and humble. The remnant of Israel will trust in the name of the LORD. They will do no wrong; they will tell no*** lies. *A deceitful tongue will not be found in their mouths. They will eat and lie down, and no one will make them afraid.... Sing, Daughter Zion; shout aloud, Israel! Be glad and rejoice with all your heart, Daughter Jerusalem! The* LORD *has taken away your punishment, he has turned back your enemy. The* LORD, *the King of Israel, is with you; never again will you fear any harm. The* LORD *your God is with you, the Mighty Warrior who saves. He will take great delight in you; in his love he will no longer rebuke you but will rejoice over you with singing.*" (Zephaniah 3:14-17)

"*But for you who revere my name, the sun of righteousness will rise with healing in its rays. And you will go out and frolic like well-fed calves. Then you will trample on the wicked; they will be ashes under the soles of your feet on the day when I act,*" *says the* LORD *Almighty.*" (Malachi 4:2-3)

"*Even the wilderness and desert will be glad in those days. The wasteland will rejoice and blossom with spring crocuses. Yes, there will be an abundance of flowers and singing and joy! The deserts will become as green as the mountains of Lebanon, as lovely as Mount Carmel or the plain of Sharon. There the* LORD *will display his glory, the splendor of our God.*" (Isaiah 35:1-4)

Jesus mentions the rewards we are to receive for our faith when He returns. "*Since you have kept my command to endure patiently, I will also keep you from the hour of trial that is going to come on the whole world to test the inhabitants of the earth. I am coming soon. Hold on to what you have, so that no one will take your crown. The one who is victorious I will make a pillar in the temple of my God.*" (Revelation 3:10-12)

And here is another blessing we can look forward to: "*The one who is victorious will, like them, be dressed in white. I will never blot out the name of that person from the book of life; but will acknowledge that name before my Father and his angels.*" (Revelation 3:5)

Final Things

*Some will ask, what happens
after the Millennium?*

We are told that after Jesus rules for 1000 years, God will burn up all of creation and that nothing will be left in existence other than His Great White Throne of Judgement. That is when all the dead who practiced evil and shunned belief and obedience to God will stand and receive their condemnation. – After that, God will create a new heaven and a new earth that shall last eternally, on which his children from among mankind throughout all ages will live forever. There are multiple verses that refer to this. "*See, I will create new heavens and a new earth. The former things will not be remembered, nor will they come to mind. Be glad and rejoice forever in what I will create.*" (Isaiah 65:17-18)

God will create a new heaven and new earth that will last forever. "*The heavens will pass away with a great noise, and the elements will melt with fervent heat, the Earth also, the works shall be burned up. The heavens being on fire and the elements shall melt with fervent heat. Since everything will be destroyed in this way, what kind of people ought you to be? You ought to live holy and godly lives as you look forward to the day of God and speed its coming. That day will bring about the destruction of the heavens by fire, and the elements will melt in the heat. But in keeping with his promise we are looking forward to a new heaven and a new earth, where righteousness dwells.*" (2 Peter 3:10-13)

Our loving Savior will never abandon us. He will be with us for all time. This little life we live now is just the beginning of an eternity of wonder, amazement, love, and delight. "*His dynasty will go on forever; his kingdom will endure as the sun. It will be as eternal as the moon, my faithful witness in the sky!*" (Psalm 89:36-37)

"*As surely as my new heavens and earth will remain, so will you always be my people, with a name that will never disappear,*" says the LORD." (Isaiah 66:22)

It has been my endeavor by writing this book to make it relevant to all believers in God from all religious faiths, including Jews, and the various divisions of Christian churches across the world. We all believe in One supreme God. A God of holiness who cares about us and desires an eternal relationship with each person reading this. I respect the sincerity of your beliefs. However, my hope is that you have read this with an open mind. I have not presented my subjective opinion; but I have only displayed succinctly and accurately what prophets selected by God, and indwelt by his Holy Spirit, have related in the Bible. – If you believe these prophecies and promises made in the name of God, then you have come to the conclusion I've hoped for. You now know that the Messiah, our heavenly Savior to come, is Jesus the Christ.

He is our great hope that provides us peace amidst chaos and turmoil. He is our assurance of a better world and eternal life. "*With this news, strengthen those who have tired hands, and encourage those who have weak knees. Say to those with fearful hearts, "Be strong, and do not fear, for your God is coming to destroy your enemies. He is coming to save you.*" (Isaiah 35:3-4)

I close with a plea made by Jesus to you: "**Behold, I stand at the door and knock. If anyone hears My voice and opens the door, I will come in and dine with him, and he with Me.**" (Revelation 3:20) Invite Him into your heart, mind, and soul.

"There is salvation in no one else, for there is no other name under heaven given among men by which we must be saved." (Acts 4:12)

~ Mark Baird ~

About the Author

Mark Baird lives in San Diego, CA. He runs a charity for US Military, Veterans and their families called Patriotic Hearts. He received the calling to be a pastor in his youth. The first church in which he pastored was in Isla Vista, where 20,000 students live attending the University of Santa Barbara. The church began with 25 people and was at 400 when Mark left for his hometown of Laguna Beach where he fostered another church. He was also the Youth pastor in his town's Presbyterian Church. At this time, the Vietnam War was raging. That is when Mark received his call to serve US Veterans. Mark had tried to join the US Marines; but he was disqualified due to a medical condition. So, he has continued to serve those who served in his place ever since.

Mark's primary talents are Preaching and Teaching. He is available to do so at your church too. And where he cannot be, Mark has written such books as this to serve in his stead. More Than Conquerors: Living A Believer's Life was written prior to this book. – Mark's ministry emphasis is to prepare people for the immanent return of the Messiah.

Made in the USA
Columbia, SC
26 July 2023